RUTH FAINLIGHT

Somewhere Else Entirely

BLOODAXE BOOKS

ISBN: 978 1 78037 438 3

First published 2018 by
Bloodaxe Books Ltd,
Eastburn,
South Park,
Hexham,
Northumberland NE46 1BS.

www.bloodaxebooks.com
For further information about Bloodaxe titles
please visit our website and join our mailing list
or write to the above address for a catalogue

Supported using public funding by
ARTS COUNCIL
ENGLAND

Cover design: Neil Astley & Pamela Robertson-Pearce.

Printed in Great Britain by Bell & Bain Limited, Glasgow, Scotland, on
acid-free paper sourced from mills with FSC chain of custody certification.

ACKNOWLEDGEMENTS

Acknowledgements are due to the editors of the following publications in which some of these poems first appeared: *Acumen, Bookmark Poems,* ed. Julian Nangle (Words Press, 2015), *The Hudson Review, Hwaet: 20 Years of Ledbury Poetry Festival,* ed. Mark Fisher (Bloodaxe Books/Ledbury Poetry Festival, 2016), *Jubilee Lines: 60 Poets for 60 Years,* ed. Carol Ann Duffy (Faber & Faber, 2012), *New Humanist, 1914: Poetry Remembers,* ed. Carol Ann Duffy (Faber & Faber, 2014), *Ploughshares* (USA), *Poem, Roundyhouse, The Times Literary Supplement,* and *Wretched Strangers,* ed. Ágnes Lehóczky & J.T. Welsch (Boiler House Press, 2018).

CONTENTS

Meditations on Yellow

Morning sunlight streaking through the blind
lit the jagged scratch from a roller-skate
in the kitchen floor's jazz-patterned lino
which I filled with putty and tried to hide
with my art-school oil-paints in every shade
of tan and brown, cream and yellow.

Yellow batter my aunt would swirl
– as if the gesture granted magical power –
in the mixing bowl tilted at an angle;
the acid-yellow of her lemon meringue.
Pallid chicken feet made the soup gelatinous,
discs of golden fat floating on its surface.

Such glowing yellow: the colour
of a slice of corn bread, toasted, spread
with canary-yellow butter, cheddar
cheese or thick amber honey.
That greeny glint on a flask
of vivid gamboge-yellow olive oil.

Clusters of mimosa, its powdery yellow
flower-heads hardening into grainy globes,
sprouted from the pewter-smooth boughs
of the tree outside our house in France.
Later we found a grove of them, and you
thinned it out for the cooking stove.

Yellow of the daffodils I helped my friend
to pick, then carefully wrap in tissue paper
for the man who bought them. After staring
down the trumpets of hundreds, what revulsion
I felt at the repetition of sepal and stamen,
all that mechanism of reproduction.

The Fiat Eco Panda was custard yellow.
In the slow lane on the motorway I came
closest to death when a white van smashed
into the side of your car and I ricocheted
like a crash dummy. But we both stepped,
resurrected, from the crumpled yellow metal.

This morning, walking down the mews,
I peeled fallen leaves off the damp cobbles:
amber, copper, cordovan tan,
all the autumn yellows. Some were soft
as chamois gloves or straw-coloured silk,
others crisp as starched cotton.

'High yellow': politically incorrect;
but where I grew up, meant a beautiful girl
with African, English, Native American
and probably Chinese and Mexican, blood.
My lineage (barring some pogroms), is simple:
Ashkenazy unmixed. Just right for a yellow star.

Yellow was the colour of those curtains
my dear friend gave me. A slubbed heavy
silk of sulphurous Buddhist yellow.
So long ago: that child-murder, self-murder.
Sad beautiful creatures, mother and daughter,
two wraiths on the far shore of Lethe.

Yellow is the flaring solar centre
you must not stare into – or be
forever blind as Oedipus, or cursed
as mad king Croesus: who starved
to death when all he touched,
child, flower or food, hardened to gold.

Late Spring Evening in the Suburbs

Late spring: lilac, wisteria, laburnum.
Mauve, pink, lemon-yellow. Tender clouds.
Sunday in the suburbs. Last night, next-door
lit their barbeque. Windows alert!
The smell of charring meat clings to the curtains
and the sliding door of the kitchen extension
had to be closed, fast. But they are good neighbours
and uncomplainingly shut their windows
to muffle the new CD of Courtney Barnett
singing her songs and playing her guitar
that we listen to while chopping vegetables
for one of David's mutton curries.
I can hear children in other gardens.
This fine weather means spectacular sunsets.
The waning moon rides high above the rooftops.
In houses opposite, the lights go on.

The Ides of March

The Ides of March. Tomorrow, full moon.
Now, blue sky and a few clouds, the air
sweet and mild: the year's best day.
Every tree and bush in the square,
leaves and petals tender and glossy,
is budding, sprouting, blossoming.

How awful if all this growth
were shrivelled and burnt by cold, if
the temperature dropped and the hard
winter threatened finally does arrive.

Imagining, I become a farmer, staring
across his fields, newly ploughed and sown,
already dusted with green growth.
It cannot but delight – although
he know it's too early in the season,
and if the weather turns, there's nothing
he can do to protect those seedlings.

Stiff with dread, the farmer thinks of God,
but how often that god has failed him.
His God is as helpless as he.
(He must be a very minor god
who cannot even control the weather.)

Somewhere on the other side of the universe
lives the Master God, the God of gods,
and whatever happens in the millions
of solar systems spangled through space,
on the tens of millions of planets,
is done by his will and for his pleasure.

To understand him, remember
your own pleasure watching hundreds of ants
desperately working to shore up

the structure shattered when you lifted a stone
heedlessly from the side of the road
and all their effort crumbled;
how you diverted yourself further
by laying a straw across their path:

this is what the Master God must feel
when floodwaters swirl, volcanos erupt
and the earth moves and opens; when
thousands of creatures – human, minute,
indistinguishable – wailing and beating
their breasts, fall onto their knees to pray.

Meanwhile, Brutus and Caesar wait
in the wings to act their fated roles,
and a cold front of low pressure
approaches from northeast. The moon
begins to wane. The Master God,
as ever, is an absorbed spectator.

The Motorway

I was born in the motorway era:
we both were. He used to say it made him
happy to see me writing in the car,
in the passenger seat.

We drove the motorways – going north on
the M1, all the routes through France heading south,
west from Nashville to San Diego, north
to San Francisco, then east again
across the continent to Montauk Point,
you driving, me writing.

Sometimes I'd be aware you'd quickly turned
your head sideways, only for a moment
shifting your gaze from the road – one flick
of your eyes, to watch me making notes.
I laughed and said: 'It's perfect: you driving,
me writing, let's go on like this forever,'
and you smiled and agreed.

But we didn't. There were other things to do.
And now it's impossible. You're dead.
And I'm driving with another person,
with someone else.

I stare through the windscreen into the distance
as the pylons draw their lines of power
across the green and brown and yellow fields,
the landscape of small hills, hedges and streams
you taught me to understand – stare into
the distance – as if by looking hard enough
I'll find that place where the two sides
of the road meet and unite.

In the Square

1 *Snowdrops*

At the top of the square, the furthest you could walk
last spring, those last few weeks before they took
you to hospital, you'd stop at the same bench,
marked with the name of someone who'd lived nearby,
whose friends wanted him to be remembered.

I'd leave you there to make my daily circuit
past the playground and the tennis courts,
but look back from every turning. Thin face,
white beard, hat pulled low, scarf around his neck,
no doubt at all: that gaunt, old man was sick.

It's nine months since your death, but I still
see you seated on that bench whenever I pass,
as potent a presence as these firm, bright green
stalks and leaves pushing up through the cold earth.

And now you point towards the first snowdrops.

II *The Choice*

Why am I always tired,
why can't I sleep?
Why, every few hours,
all through the night,
do I wake with a start.
I'm grieving.
(Hard to believe
it took almost two years
to acknowledge the obvious.)

I walk around the square
sit down on the same bench
where...almost two years...
The cold clear air
the weak winter sun
on my face... Now I could sleep...
The hum of birds and planes
and cars lulling me deeper
as if sliding into a lake
of freezing water. The choice
between whether to sink or
push toward the further shore
has already been made.

Oxygen Mask

What happened that afternoon? I cannot
remember: no clear sound of your voice,
not one single word or gesture
remain as evidence to ponder
from what I did not know
was the last time I would see you alive.

Ordinary desultory talk;
your room was warm, though only April.
There was another visitor, so
nothing personal was said, nothing
to prick the memory like a burr
you cannot tear from inside your shirt.
Better such pain than a vacant mind
with no power of recall.

I could scream: which might stop me reliving,
over and over, what happened next:
how the shrill phone dragged me from sleep
in the small hours; how I did not arrive
in time; how your hand stiffened and chilled
in mine and your face paled; how I pushed
aside the oxygen mask though the nurse
who brought me a drink had said to leave it
so your jaw would not drop – I remember that.
And then the final kiss.

Alan's Jacket

A photograph in *The New Yorker* of Elvis Presley and Sam Phillips, the founder of Sun Records in Memphis, Tennessee and the man who discovered Presley. But the most important fact is that the picture was taken in 1956, and the tweed jacket Phillips is wearing, and the two men's short glossy hair (brilliantined, surely) remind me so strongly of Alan. He was partial to similar tweed jackets in the mid-fifties, sometimes put brilliantine on his hair, and had the same air of youthful confidence and swagger. The jacket isn't really like any Alan wore, which were of various tweeds but not this particular pattern; it must be the shape, the boxy fifties cut. It didn't take long, though, for Alan's jackets to lose their original appearance. Both pockets bulged and dragged, filled with all his smoker's paraphernalia: a pouch or tin of tobacco and a box of Swan Vesta matches on one side, a curved briar pipe and the instrument for cleaning it out on the other, apart from whatever else he might carry in them.

The two men in the photograph are totally absorbed by the guitar, which hangs from Presley's left shoulder but is being pulled slightly forward and held by Phillips, who is plucking the strings with his right hand; and I suddenly notice that Presley has not let the other man take over: his left hand is curved around the neck of the instrument and half covers Phillips' fingers. That assertion of control and his downcast concentrated gaze also make me think of Alan. No one could ever distract him or make him do what he did not want to.

Somewhere Else Entirely

Where did you sleep last night,
where did you sleep? I feel
we spent the night together,
but when I wake, always
earlier than the alarm
is set, you're never here.
Strange, the empty bed.

I scan the other rooms
and though I seem to remember
an evening like one of hundreds
of evenings spent together –
so many years together –
peaceful evenings, each
of us at our desk, the sense
of someone else in the flat,
you in your room; then
going to bed: affection,
embraces, intimacy....

Now everything is different.
I walk along the hall,
enter each room, uneasy,
seeking, but find no sign....
Although every room
retains so many memories,
sounds and images, is
saturated with your essence,
I know I'll never meet you here....

Where you sleep, day and night,
is dark and cold and silent:
somewhere else entirely.

A Meeting with My Dead

I'm alone in the house and suddenly feel
the need to phone my mother. But it's decades
since she died – and I don't remember
having this urge before. Something altered.
Now, for the first time in thirty years
she wanted her daughter, and I want to talk
to them: mother, father, brother, husband:
all my dead. But what do I want to ask them?

Like a glass of water, darkened by one drop
of ink, I am suffused by unexpected thoughts.
Their realm and my world have no connection.
They have forgotten almost everything.
I look into my mother's eyes – they are calm
and seem paler, her gaze is barely focussed
but she is smiling; all of them are smiling.
As far as I can judge, they are happy –

although I'm not certain that they recognise me.
And where exactly are we? Is this puffy
stuff the floor of Heaven? Now I notice:
the four are dressed in suspiciously similar
clothes, which could be robes, and those books
they hold look holy. Then they start to sing:
a sanctimonious droning counterpoint.
It makes me anxious. Might I be dead as well?

I look down at an unfamiliar garment
(I seem to be wearing a nightdress):
does this mean that I've joined the family choir?
I love them, and I'm old enough, for sure –
but I feel it's far too soon to die.
At last I know the question, but realise
they'll never give an answer. The phone rings.
I'm awake, at my desk. My throat tightens.

Froth

End of the working day, end of the winter.
Everyone I see looks convalescent,
smutched and nerve-worn.

Faces on the escalator jolt past
like peaks of dirty froth
sluiced through gratings into a sealed-off river.

The slightest shift of pressure was enough
to shape each cheek or nostril:
variations of the potter's thumb.

Sand

A loosely cupped hand,
and through the lax fingers
slides brownish grey sand

so dry that dust rises
to blur the air between
hand and pensive eye

of the one who looks, amazed
by how completely what
was borne a thousand days

became intolerable.
And the confirmation
that this clear knowledge,

suddenly insistent
as the beating of a trapped
insect's fluttering wings

against the window's glass,
is valid? Not a smudge of sand
is left on the palm of that hand.

Torsion

The sigh and scratch and drag
the rustle and swish
– like the hiss of surf
down a shingle beach
as the tide pulls back,
or the flutter and creak
of pallid plumes and quills
on a white peacock's fan
as it unfurls,
spiralling...

...the sigh and scratch and drag
from the train on a narrow dress
heavy with metal beads,
vitreous glint
and gunmetal glow,
scraping along the floor
then nudged aside by
the tip of a velvet toe
as the music starts
for the next dance:
spiralling waltz,
torsion of tango.

Numinous

The earth is turning on its axis:
all day long I feel the room,
the house, the street, slide
slowly sideways,
clockwise
north to south
east to west:
as dignified as a Cunard liner
keel parting foaming water
released into its element.

Almost impossible to ignore
once I sense the planet's movement,
that unstoppable gyration.
The thought is dizzying.
My fingers
want to dig into the earth
clutch at every pebble
anything solid
not to be spun off
this suddenly unstable surface.

Then daily life's reality
reasserts. Gone,
that total
immediate, bodily, yet
numinous
consciousness
of the universal rhythm.
Now, once more, the sun proceeds
obedient from window to window.
The ground is solid under my feet.

Magic

Like a sudden veering in direction when
two surfaces shear past each other
disturb the deep strata expose a startling
yet inherent pattern

unexpected actions and demands
induce   reveal   new aspects of being
though today's calmness seems no truer
than last week's tearful panic

and though the features of her uncertain face
keep altering   in the struggle to define
one sure purpose and identity
and make it happen

no attempt as yet was potent enough
to work such magic.

Empty Space

The curdling of what should be empty
space in the darkness through the doorframe:
it clots, coagulates and coalesces
into organic matter like cloudy
masses of seething ectoplasm.

You hardly dare peer through to the next
room, or risk a move into further
dimensions, a plunge into Sleeping Beauty's hedge:
branches and stems plaited to form an almost
impassable barrier between two realms.

Now your face and hands are scratched, as if
your familiar, that cream-coloured elegant
Abyssinian cat, in an inexplicable
change of mood, hissing, snarling and twisting
out of your arms, were suddenly possessed.

You can't remember where you are: which
phase of your life, which house, at this moment,
you inhabit or who you live with; don't
know what animates that empty space, nor
whose ghost beckons through the open door.

Regret

The move not made
The step not taken
The gesture of comfort delayed
past the crucial moment...
The stifled caress...
Corrosive regret.

Wonderful

The first lines of this poem
must be hidden
somewhere among the phrases
written on these scraps of paper
(all I could find in the early hours):
words about poetry.

I'd promised that boy
he could come to my office later
to talk about his poem.
This was a dream: I was younger
than now – but he was even younger.
I wanted to tell him
I was working on a poem
so would not be able to meet him,
to tell him that for me
poetry was more important
than anything else.

I think that in the dream
I was his teacher, or mentor.
I kissed him to make sure
he would never forget this lesson
(transgressive, forbidden, I know,
kissing a student),
so that it would stay with him forever.
'Yes, go and write your poem,' he said,
half admiring, half bitter.
They were wonderful kisses.

The Red Shirt

The red of these poppy petals
and their texture are exactly
as I imagine the fabric:

pellucid Indian silk
reflecting the light from its surface
like moving water: for the shirt

with the ruffled collar touching
the soft hairs at the back of your neck
and red ruffles pushing out

from the front of your waistcoat
so you look like a flamenco dancer:
the shirt you'd flaunt.

Blind Love

Love is not blind – Love
loves what she sees:
the being in front of her eyes.

Love sees most clearly of all:
most deeply, completely and
totally loves the being she sees

before crushing the loved one
hard against her breast:
too close to be seen.

Inside a Yellow Laburnum Tent...

Inside a yellow laburnum tent
which the rain barely penetrates,
behind a screen of white lilac,
I want to hide.

Queen Anne's lace and borage
tangle in the foliage
of the lower branches,
showering blue and silver petals.

Fallen chestnut blossom
on the pebbled path
has the reddish colour of raw meat
or scabs on schoolboys' knees.

Stooping, I see the fresh
flowers rest on yesterday's petals:
darkening, softening,
mulching into the gravel.

Almost every bud and frill
of tiny crumpled leaves,
crimson and iridescent green,
shows the carnal flush of new life.

Chestnut in Spring

Tumescent chestnut buds
unsheath sticky husks
unfold a fan of glossy
embryonic leaves, and
stems and twigs thrust out
toward the sun their freight
of blossom: crumpled
coral-crimson silk
unpleating from the centre
where the new growth opens
like the spreading fingers
of a hand relaxing,
or the limbs of lovers.

Chestnut

Don't think of them as someone else's
daughters and sons, but your own
children. The tenderness of boys.
The tenderness of girls. Think of them

like still-unfurling fans of crumpled
chestnut leaves, rosy scribbles
on a blue translucent sky,
a message in April's easy code.

Remember this, when the chestnuts'
candles have gone, the children grown,
the chestnuts started to fall,

and groves of trees press close,
darkening into labyrinths
of dusty August murder-green.

The Playground

One September morning
under the willow tree's green-tasselled tent
that straddled dripping bushes and puddled path
we sheltered from an equinoctial storm
dragging heaps of yellow leaves across the grass,

then in the empty playground
saw abandoned toys: trucks, buckets, spades,
their primary colours glistened from the sandpit,
jaunty wooden snails to ride like magic horses
and two square swings like small security cages.

The slick shine of rain
gouged the bed of a river down the metal slide.
Only the roundabout, its bright red struts and
central hub a science-fiction spaceship, hinted
that above the cloud stretched endless blue sky.

Ladbroke Square Notes

The empty tennis court surrounded by darkening autumn trees, the empty wooden bench inside, small heaps of leaves piled up by the wind around the edge of the wire net fencing. I can see one abandoned ball, a damp yellowy green, the same colour streaked across some of the fallen leaves.

An Italian au pair with a sleeping boy in a pushchair and a petulant little girl whom she keeps telling – in Italian – not to pull berries off the shrubs. I wonder if the child can understand what she says.

London plane trees: *Platanus hispanica*. One is enormous, the lower part of its trunk twisted and knotted as scar tissue, gnarled as Jimmy Durante's nose. About ten feet up it divides into three secondary trunks, quite smooth and healthy looking.

Tiny children wearing bright plastic bicycle helmets, their heads enlarged until they look like cartoon ants.

The great chestnut tree on the east lawn with a wide circle of rusty leaves below, blotched and shrivelled by the disease which is devastating trees all over the country. But there seem to be as many nuts as ever, the fuzzy husks broken in half by their fall, exposing a creamy white lining. The smooth nuts, their rich henna conker colour like heads of shining hair, have tumbled out to lie among the leaves, husks, stones and mud strewn across the lawn.

The Jungle

Sweetheart,
I'm even importing you into my dreams.
The beetles were green, the parrots were green
and between the trunks of moss-swathed trees
lianas swung. But we never had been
in the jungle together. It was just a dream.

Sweetheart, another dream.
With you in a room on the upper floor
of an empty house in the far north
left derelict by a gang of squatters: torn
curtains, broken chairs, stained walls.
But we were happy and closed the door

(the dream went on) – to dull
the moans and screams, the heavy thuds
from the cellar, where a woman slumped
on a heap of dusty coal, and her brothers
or her husband's brothers (more like thugs
than tribal elders) punished her.

Sweetheart, I was frightened.
That woman was me. I was the one
who had transgressed and been judged,
the rebel ignoring ancient injunctions
who lay now in the arms of her beloved
as if in the heart of the jungle.

Then the dream ended. Yet I remember
every detail, as we lie here in bed,
can still hear their cruel words wishing
me dead, feel those blows to my head.
Sweetheart, I wonder if we shall ever
get back to that green jungle.

The Log

...a half-rotten log
on the muddy bank of a wide river
in a tropical forest
which I nudge and ease and push
with much effort
until enough of its length
is in the water, and the laws
of physics and matter take over....

no need to question
the motive for the actions,
why the log was cut
its destination or further purpose,
only to feel the pleasure and triumph
as the river's force is confirmed
and dense-grained heavy wood
slides into the deep water
is caught by the current
becomes weightless
spins and floats and turns....

Westward Streaming Cloud

The sun is pale as a moon,
and westward streaming clouds
 like skirts of grey tulle

that swirl around a dancer's
limbs, one moment hide,
the next reveal; and where

the last hard snow still lies,
packed by the wind under rocks,
under shrubs and trees, with a white

gleam as if bare flesh shone
through: it could be the moon
through westward streaming cloud.

Venus

(to Sandro Botticelli)

What made the grit in the oyster
that formed beautiful Venus,
who came floating shoreward
on an oyster shell, her flesh
as lustrous as the orient
on a royal pearl?

Some say she was engendered
by the fertilising foam
of blood and semen
from the severed genitals
of Uranus. Some,
that the pulpy tissue
inside a mollusc is
like a vulva, and the pearl,
a clitoris. Whichever,
whether flesh or nacre,
the lucky one finds treasure.

Coquillage

(to Katsushika Hokusai)

He was acting the octopus:
though better not explain
in greater detail just
what he was doing with
each pulpy probing tip
and sucker to that body,
smooth and glowing as
if buffed by powdered
oyster shell, arching
as if under foamy jets
of water, except to say:
like Japanese coquillage
it was delicious.

Hunter's Moon

The blanched glare
of a full moon
through frosted glass
on the bathroom floor

at four a.m.
as I stumble out
from tangled sheets
and an airless room

down the corridor
with parched throat
blistered mouth
to gulp water

slake and soothe
the icy thirst
the x-ray scorch
the alum burn

where the scabbed lips
and forked tongue
of the hunter's moon
seared their brand.

At the Allotment

Pink roses, blue borage and
purple thistle-heads of artichokes,
red flowers of runner beans;
small plots, dense with growth,
like an embroidered patchwork quilt.

The man at the next allotment
is netting his courgettes, while overhead,
a helicopter circles, as if the police
are searching for something or someone
in the grid of city streets.

But the beans have barely begun
to form in their pods, nor the beetroot
to swell into globes underground.
A late summer: the year-disc curving
downwards, past the solstice.

Today the connexions seem even stronger:
watching you dig and bend; pushing
my fingers through crumbling earth; dozing
in that old wonky deck chair, behind
the half-closed door of the allotment shed.

Ars Anatomica

(Number ten of a series of prints by Leonard Baskin)

I thought the drawing showed a trellis
behind a clump of iris
that should have been thinned last autumn

or was it an elbow joint
humerus radius ulna
torn tissue flayed muscle
shadowy scapula and clavicle
below the x-ray's surface

like the limp stems and pulpy purple
flower heads of overgrown iris
like bruises staining the flesh
of hip and shoulder when I tripped
and fell and broke the garden trellis.

Aloe

(from a mezzotint by Judith Rothchild)

Through burred, dense black
a ghostly aloe

with lance-sharp,
succulent flecked leaves

like an animal's pelt
(its rough guard-hairs

their spiny margin)
presses closer

against the bevel
to escape the darkness.

NOTES:

Line 1: the word 'burred' is specifically used in reference to the technique of abrading the metal plate for the mezzotint with a burin (name of the tool used).

Lines 6 & 7: 'guard hairs' are the longer, coarser hairs of an animal's pelt which protect the softer, denser fur beneath.

World Events

Nineteen sixty-three: Kennedy is
assassinated, the Beatles release their first
album, and Valentina Tereshkova
floats weightless against a faint radiation
from the final remnants of the Big Bang:
the first woman in space.

I had to Google 'world events' for that year,
but there was no problem remembering
what I'd been doing.

We travelled back from Morocco, because
Alan was invited to Russia, and now that Ted
had left her, Sylvia and I planned to spend
that month together in North Tawton
 with our three babies (and my nanny
to make it possible), talking, walking,
and writing poetry.

I was the new mother: my son a few months
the younger; but she already had a daughter,
plus a published first collection – which made
me feel competitive, and I didn't like that! –
although she envied my 'glamorous life',
she confessed. But we acknowledged so much
in common, with delight.

That poetic meeting never happened, yet
I dream about it. What more to say? Everyone
knows the story's ending.

Credit cards, Valium, cassette tapes,
remote controls for TV: developments
of nineteen sixty-three. And more events.
Now each protagonist of this sad tale,
bar me, is dead – yet all of us are blessed:
we live through poetry.

Time and Function

I function on geological time.
Five thousand years seems a moment
to me, the blink of an eyelid.
I belong with the rocks not the ants.

I function on cosmological time.
I feel comfortable with the concept
of aeons. I know that space is not empty.
Dark matter is my element.

I function on biological time:
dark pulpy tissue, veins and
sinews, glistening muscle fibres.
I am a mortal animal.

Timeless Waters

Thinking about time: wondering
how much time is left: whether
it's time to start detaching   time
to clear: ah yes, clear
                         clear water

To drink a glass of clear water
float on a green and blue ocean:
the feel of water   the movement
of water
          against my skin

Is this what death will be like:
return to that warm amniotic
fluid   return to the ocean:
to those timeless
                         waters of life.

Continuation

I am going to live forever.
I don't know if my bones will last forever
or my various systems hold out: probably not:
but I shall, whatever happens to them.

It came with absolute conviction, when
I woke up this morning but lay for a while in bed:
even though I cannot explain how I knew,
what I mean, or why I am so confident.

It has nothing to do with God, or Heaven.
It won't be an afterlife but continuation of
exactly the same as the present. Anything else
is unthinkable. I refuse to imagine an end.

The Next Station

A new sensation.
A strong emotion.
Spasms of anger.
Regret about wasted effort,
wasted time and wasted life.

Another victory
for traditional wisdom,
another confirmation.
This was supposed to happen.
Nothing can change it.

It's just the next station
along the road or
down the line
before the tunnel.
Almost the destination.

Petulant

The same thought, almost since I can remember,
rejecting movement, action, pleasure:
What is the point of doing/going/seeing etc,
something or other,
if I can't live forever?

The Poet's Funeral

Clouds sagged over the sodden fields
like elephants collapsing.
Through the cold church an incense odour
of heaped lilies,
        while a Jesus-dolly,
white-haired and surpliced, ululated
over the coffin. The widow's rigid back
as she followed it out.
        Her black veil.

Daisy

The ultra-violet vision of a honey bee
sees the centre of a daisy as red, not yellow.
My version is the wrong colour,
unrelated to the flower's purpose:
a thought which begs so many questions.

One of which might be if 'beauty' and 'nature'
have other connections than pleasure
to a power that functions by metaphor.
Another (let's forget the honey bee):
can my view of the world resemble yours?

Thought-forms

Form is the vehicle for thought.
The shifting of muscle and bone
into gesture and expression
is all I can know of your soul:
every thought creates its own form.

Underground

Over and over, scrolling across the indicator
in letters of neon green: 'Person under a train.
No service between Liverpool Street and Leytonstone'.
Avoiding each others' eyes, we wait on the platform.

It's almost always a young woman who stands up
to give me a seat. Men, whatever their age, mothers
whose children could sit on their laps instead of beside
them, stare ahead, indifferent or self-righteous.

A soberly dressed Chinese couple, swaying
against the doors, are trying to hold a sturdy,
rosy, wriggling toddler, vivid in pink sweatshirt,
red leggings and orange satin slippers.

At Oxford Circus, the message is softened.
The indicator merely states: 'Passenger accident
at Stratford', as the child slides out of their arms
and runs to the other end of the carriage.

At Baker Street Underground Station

Until now, they've kept
between the tracks, but last night –

was it the full moon
so emboldened them? –

they were there on the platform,
setting empty beercans rolling

rattling crumpled wrappers
under the chocolate machine and

running behind the benches,
almost over my feet.

Elementary

I

Hurricane   Earthquake   Conflagration   Flood:
the elements at their most destructive.

Zephyr, flowery meadow, hearth and pond:
their mildest, most benign embodiment.

The essence of elemental matter
however it chooses to manifest

is the spirit that rides the waves' surface
howls from the radiant centre of the furnace

or sliding under oceanic alps, channels
sediments into mineral strata.

II

Elementary, my dear Watson, how could
you think otherwise? Human pride always

denies the likelihood of disaster.
Move yourself uptown immediately,

before the levees fail and tunnels fill
with sewer water. You can take my word,

it's bound to happen soon, that I know.
So put your books on the top shelf, your gold

in the bank vault, your furs into storage. But still
expect the worst. You won't be disappointed.

A Republican Tale

The Ominous Onion
was flashing 'Exceptional Convoy'
as it pushed to the front of the crowd.
This onion knew its stuff:
onions are as good
as anyone else,
and its papery skin,
thin as gold-leaf,
its crisp, silvery flesh,
far outdid other magnificence.

When the two prancing greys
pulling the Royal coach
saw the ringed stripes,
diagonal red and white,
of his trousers and jacket –
each button flashing
'Exceptional Convoy' –
and above them, the Onion's ominous
republican smile,
they reared back,
the coach crashed,
and all the princesses and princes
inside, tumbled out, giggling.

Floor-walker

Her father was a floor-walker:
every night for years, up and
down the worn-linoleumed hall,
another screaming infant in his arms;
by day, up and down the aisles
under the sulphurous yellow lights
of a small-town general store.

It could have been Peoria, Piura,
or Puri, because the only job
for girls, when she left school,
was maid or waitress. There was never
a shortage of that sort of work.
But she was ambitious – thought
she'd find her fortune in the city.

Soon, she was part of a group (you
can imagine the set-up: failed
students, blocked artists,
the excitement of a false address,
arrests, interrogations and
denials). She learned a lot, but
other situations taught her more.

Then the redirected letter came –
too late for the funeral. She was glad
he hadn't lived to know that though
you could say she followed in his foot-
steps (but walking asphalt not lino),
his daughter was a whore. Her mother
had cried her eyes out long before.

But all her life she'd been in thrall
to the same delusive image which
had warped his existence, that false
ideal for which her friends were
still being questioned and tortured.
It was awful. She had to get out.
She dreamed she'd save them all.

Male and Female Created He Them

I

Standing, all of us jammed close together
in the rush hour, they don't notice me watching,
inches away. They are young and healthy
but, apart from the glow of emotion,
exceptionally plain. The resemblance
between them is striking: blond, in glasses and
raincoats, clutching briefcases. They probably
work in the same building: banking, insurance,
and travel the same line daily. (It seemed
like an omen, being neighbours already.)
They may not get married at once, but soon
will be sharing a mortgage. Something about them
makes me certain they are going to be happy:
floods me with envy.

II

On a train, in the street,
at the opera house,
looking at the faces,

I always wonder which one
when disaster comes
will pass the test
and save me.

What Ails Thee, Santa?

Oh what can ail thee, Santa Claus,
woebegone instead of jolly?
It might be said you look almost
off your trolley.

Oh what can ail thee, Santa Claus?
You have a job, though times are hard,
in this well-heated shopping mall.
Thank your lucky stars.

So stretch a smile across your face,
get back into Santa's grotto,
check your beard is still in place,
then coax that toddler

toward your lap, to hotly breathe
into your ear her present-list.
She slides off, happy. The next seems
more suspicious –

but you win him over. Morning,
afternoon, it doesn't matter.
Still another month to Christmas.
What ails thee, Santa?

Madame Lavitte

Last year, when Madame Lavitte
gave a tea-party for a few neighbours
on her eightieth birthday, she was so lively,
with jokes and stories about her youth
in the wilds of French West Africa.

This year, she's in a 'house of retreat'
at Montpellier. The blind grey shutters
on the house across the street fade and
dissolve like layers of dusty net curtains
as the sun gets higher. But they still conceal

those darkened rooms where father, mother
and husband died – which afterwards
were only opened once each summer
when the children came. Her neighbours
wonder what changes those heirs will make.

Three Men

I

First, Joe, my mother's elder brother,
the clever lawyer. Clearing the house
after her death, I found two photos of him.
Their sepia tones made his face soft as
a schoolboy's — but already too sensitive.

Dressed in a collegiate robe
and mortarboard, one of the photos
seems to celebrate a graduation.
In the other, his mouth is harder
and he looks a few years older,
but just as anxious. (He was
already married and a father).

Behind him hangs a painted backdrop
of army tents and a fluttering Stars
and Stripes. But someone had been careless.
The flagpole seems to have impaled him,
rising from the top of his head.

He's wearing uniform: greatcoat
and puttees, and holds a high-crowned hat
close against his thigh. Yet I find it
hard to imagine him as a doughboy.

What happened during basic training?
I was suspicious — although never
learned exactly what led to his discharge —
but they told me that when he came home
he was different. Months later,
terrifying wife and children,
he had his first spectacular breakdown.

After a few more, he was sent
to one of those places for 'nervous diseases':
discreet, upstate, and not too expensive,
and stayed there for the rest of a long life.

II

The second man was Joe's son.
Another war had begun, and Stephen
was just old enough to be drafted.
He was sweet-natured and handsome.
I had a girlish crush on him.

It was lucky we were visiting
my aunt that day – how could we know
it was the last time we'd see him?
He had come to say goodbye to his
favourite aunt: the only family member
who would read his poems.

Then once again, the training camp:
that place of danger for him and his father.
This time, impossible to hide the facts.
He was run over by one of the same
group he'd trained with, (maybe
even a friend). Half drunk, the youth
climbed into the cab of an army truck
parked under the trees, and soon careened
out of control. Stephen, too close
to escape, was crushed to death.

III

Number three – the same scenario:
raw recruits and too much beer.
This is how my husband's uncle died –
not at the Battle of the Aisne, nor
in the senseless slaughter at Loos,
but on a moor in Norfolk. It can't
really be called collateral damage:
just boys being drunk and playful.

I never met him, but know
from stories my husband told
that Oliver was one of those youths,
gentle and kind, loved by his sisters,
and mourned until the end of their lives.
I shared the grief, pity and rage
he still felt about his uncle's fate.

Because his father was a blacksmith,
Oliver was used to horses:
so was the one ordered to lead
a string of mules across the moor
at dusk. As a joke, some of his mates
fed rum to the mules – who went wild.
Trying to control them,
a blow to the head from a hoof downed him:
they kicked him to death.
His body lay exposed on the moor
until found the next afternoon
and sent back home for burial.

War destroyed these three men
who never reached a battlefield.

They never reached a battlefield,
But War destroyed these three men.

Three men who never reached a battlefield,
but War destroyed them.

...only then

when the ropes are loosened
the gag slackened
when the current's fused
                        the implements broken

when your rescuers come
force the door of your cell
when your tormentor is caught
            and you are free

then each affront and wound
smarts more lived through again
then the pain of healing starts
                        ...only then

Them

A persistent image, recurrent through her existence: a group of women, busy efficient wives and mothers – and she is twelve or thereabouts, frantic for acknowledgement (not merely from them, who fascinate and appal, with their assumption of knowing best that what they are and what they represent – tradition, pain and death – is bound to win: the destiny that will make her one of them), but from the men,

– and how reluctantly she registers the women's complicit smiles and pitying gaze, which tacitly warn how hopeless her project is, charged with memories of their own doomed girlhood attempts and the cruel truth they were forced to accept: the men will never – or is it that they can never? – give what she wants, nor even admit that she might be of the same order and species; because for the men, the only function of women and wives (once girls change to women and women become wives, their own wives or the wives of friends) is to work their fearful filthy generative magic: to incubate more delicate new female flesh: like hers was then.

The Mother

She was the age of a mother – which is
ageless. Mothers are neither old nor young.
Their time is different than the time their children
hasten through, ignoring the present moment,
craving the future, always changing.
Mothers must stay the same and never change.

What a disappointment, a betrayal, when
you first notice her greying hair and wrinkles,
how she seems suddenly smaller and tired.
Mothers should be strong enough to survive
whatever we do to them or ourselves
and are not permitted to frighten us
with an indifferent face, nor admit
the likelihood they'll be the first to die.

The Difference

Hemming with herringbone stitches
(exquisite, almost invisible),
as small and as regular
as if sewn by that woman
who crouched for hours
close to a smoky lantern
to finish embroidering
the princess's wedding gown
before the morning,

I sit on my bed, needle flashing
in probing afternoon sunlight,
or later, like a kitchen skivvy
chopping parsley fine enough
to garnish an emperor's dish,
musing on the fact that for
the palace cook or seamstress
the only possible freedom
is to perfect their skill.

Idle thoughts. I can
choose my occupation.
I am a free person.
Although we share the same
thrill when craft
becomes art (and gratitude
for that good fortune)
I know the difference:
I can do as I wish.

Art and Action

Think about a find of gold and silver
vessels wrought in high relief:
ancient, exquisite, an emperor's
treasure; then broken, melted
for their weight as metal.

Imagine their maker ready to die,
protecting his work. And helpless,
die he did. Remember
warrior-tales of gleeful havoc –
blood and smoke and torches –

which might be another art-form
or subject for contemplation,
different versions of the battle
between spirit and matter:
a god or devil writing on the wall.

New Year Wish

Walking through the park
this clear cold afternoon
between solstice and the year's end

and seeing, on dry twigs,
under dead leaves, the soft
furred pale or raw red buds,

those knots and nubs, sparks
and beads of energy,
optimistic witnesses

to the ordinary fact
and mundane miracle
of their survival and renewal,

becomes an exercise
in ecstasy: makes me
want you to be equally blessed:

makes me
want you to be
equally blessed.

A Living Creature

The angle at which the sun filtered through the half-translucent manilla-coloured blind made a long diagonal line on the opposite wall, bisecting it into triangles of clear yellow and tender buff.

This is the earliest image I recall: a sunlit room in a Bronx apartment, when the Grand Concourse was a desirable location for aspiring young families. I was penned into the high-sided crib where my mother had left me for an afternoon nap. If I was still using the crib I could not have been more than three years old, my brother not yet born.

Earlier, I had pulled myself up by the cot's round bars of pale varnished wood to lean across its top rail and ponder my surroundings: the patterned linoleum and fluffy rug, the painted cupboard for bedding and clothes, my toy-chest, a small padded chair. Now I lay on my back, covered only by a thin sheet, my hand resting on my thigh and with a strong sense of ebbing pleasure, a consciousness of having done something that should be kept secret.

I also remember how I quickly rolled onto one side, pretending to be asleep, when I heard the door open and mother entered the room. I knew that she would regard what I had done as wrong. It was my first sense of myself as an individual living creature, not merely the infant I could recognise in the family photo album but whose image did not entirely define me. That moment of self-awareness and the memory of that realm of golden bliss has remained with me ever since. Even when it has not entered my mind for years, I have always believed it is the basis of whatever confidence and strength sustain me.

Language

My aunt Ann is working in the kitchen, cooking. Steam rises from the pans on the stove. Her printed cotton housedress is short-sleeved and low-necked, but the pale flesh of her arms and chest, her face bare of any makeup, and the cloth between her shoulder blades and under her arms are damp from the heat. I am sitting on the floor half underneath the kitchen table, almost at her feet, looking at a sample book of swatches of different-coloured fabrics which a friend of hers brought over for me to play with. No other person is part of/enters this scenario – we seem to be alone in the apartment. The men: my father and her husband Roscoe, were at work; where they went to do it and what they did, were outside my range of interest.

The two sisters, my mother Fanny and my aunt Ann, lived in neighbouring apartments in the Bronx then, although I am not sure how long this arrangement lasted, and there is no one left to tell me; but not very long, I suspect. It suited them both: they enjoyed speaking Yiddish when they were alone during the day. Neither my father nor uncle spoke or understood the language, but it was the two women's mother tongue, the idiom of their family home, the only language their parents really understood, in spite of years in the USA and the grocery store – first in Harlem and then further down the island into Manhattan – which the overworked mother ran, while her husband followed the tradition of the old country and spent his time studying Talmud and Torah and dominating the family, as well as all the neighourhood women who came into the store to buy their groceries. Or so I gathered; both those grandparents were dead before their daughters married.

The sound of my aunt's and mother's exchanges, whether murmured or raucous as they laughed together at some ridiculous memory, was the background of that time in my life. I never understood what they were saying, apart from the few interpolated English phrases, but whenever I hear it: Yiddish originally being a German dialect into which words from Hebrew and various European languages were incorporated, I always feel on the verge of being able to understand German.

Tomato

The man and the little girl are in a boat on a lake in a park in New York City. A Sunday in the 1930s, not long before the start of the Second World War. He seems in his early thirties, with dark curly hair and glasses, and has a clerkly look. She has the same curly hair; there is a strong resemblance between them.

It is an overcast day, hot and humid, and the man soon stops rowing, sighs, and lets the oars slip into their locks. His shirt sticks to his back and sweat makes his moustache itch. The girl, who is about four years old, notices how the water seems to dimple down where the blade of the oar enters then rise up on each side, like a spoon dipped into a bowl of half-set Jello. There is hardly any more colour on the water than in the pale sky or the grey asphalt at the lake's edge and the faded patches of late summer grass on the low horizon which is all she can see from where they float. The only vivid colours in sight are in her cotton dress, with its complicated checked pattern of spinach green, beetroot red, and white, which reminds her of yesterday's lunch: a poached egg on a mound of spinach. Today, Mummy is at home with the baby, and she and Daddy are going to have a picnic in the park.

Spinach is good and so is beetroot, but she hates tomatoes, especially when they are over-ripe, like the one he takes from the brown paper sack containing their lunch. There are also some soggy egg and mayonnaise sandwiches and a few cookies.

The boat lies motionless in the centre of the small lake, surrounded by still water with the tone and weight of quicksilver. There are no other boats near them. He feels that they are very close to the water, like insects resting on its surface.

In the food bag, the man finds a twist of waxy paper holding salt. He spreads the various ingredients of their picnic on the empty seat between them, then cuts the tomato into two halves, sprinkles them with salt, and holds one out.

'I don't like tomato,' the girl says, but he repeats the gesture. She refuses again. Again he stretches his long arm, his enormous hand, the glistening, oozing, salt-crusted tomato towards her, until it is almost under her nose. She senses that he is beginning to lose his temper.

'I don't want it.' 'Take it from me, right now, take it, I say.' 'I don't want it.' 'You'll do what I tell you, or else...' 'I won't, I won't, I hate tomato!'

It has become imperative to make her obey, but he realises that he cannot even stand up in the boat without the risk of capsizing. A wave of helpless exasperation surges through him so powerfully that he imagines pushing his daughter into the lake or plunging below the surface himself.

The girl is shocked and flustered by her father's insistence, though not enough to stop her from repeating stubbornly, 'I hate tomato. I hate salt.' The slimy white-scabbed object so near her face is making her feel sick.

With a violent, sudden movement he leans forward, grasps her shoulder with his free hand, and smears the tomato against her mouth. She splutters, spits, twists her head sideways and – her action even swifter than his – pulls the tomato out of his hand and away from her mouth, and throws it into the water. A plume of salt spirals to the surface as it disappears under the boat.

She is frightened. He is ashamed. For several minutes they stare dumbly at each other, hearts pounding. He is the one who turns his gaze away first, then slowly levers the oars into position and rows toward the shore.

The Grand Concourse

I think my parents were living in the Bronx, on or near the Grand Concourse, when I was born. It is too late now to establish the facts: it was only after they both had died that I wanted to check this, as well as hundreds of other details about my first few years of life. (I discover that most people feel they have made the same mistake.) There are photographs of me in a park wearing a pretty little sunsuit, looking about two years old, probably taken and obviously printed by a professional photographer, and on the back of each shiny page is an address on the Grand Concourse. Something about the narrow strip of park lawn visible behind me made me think I remembered it: a palimpsest of sensory evocations: one memory overlaying the one beneath, different visits to park and playground each leaving its separate yet similar trace, and a sufficient number of them to authenticate the experience – which led to the conclusion that for some time we had indeed lived on, or near, the Grand Concourse.

The Grand Concourse: such an intriguing address! The photographs I found online did not display the grandeur I thought its name demanded, although it was modelled on the Champs-Élysées, and there was a stern plainness to the wide boulevard. In the early years of the twentieth century, that part of the Bronx was changing from farmland to residential property, and the new apartment blocks (many of them splendid examples of art deco) built for the children of the previous generation of immigrants who were moving up from the crowded tenements of the East End, offered 'spacious accommodation on the Park Avenue of middle-class Bronx residents'.

In the 1970s and 80s I was often in Canada and the USA, to read my poems at festivals and colleges, and to spend periods of time at various universities. In New York, I would stay with my cousin Fanny in the family apartment on Riverside Drive. She was a widow now, but her still unmarried brother and son lived there with her. When my mother, brother and I had left the States in 1946 to go back to England and my father after a six-year separation due to the Second World War, I remember being in that same apartment to say goodbye to Fanny, and her husband, teenaged son (he was a few years older than me), bachelor brother and retired parents, who all lived there. Only Frank, who was married, had left home. I did not know that it would be twenty five years until my next visit to New York.

Those were the worst years for the Bronx: arsonists were devastating the borough, and landlords burning down their own properties for the insurance money. I did not want to believe that the riot and chaos reached as far as the Grand Concourse – but news photos on my computer showed the wide roadway jammed with fire engines and black smoke curling from top-floor windows. One weekend I was visiting my friend Kathy on Long Island. She had promised to drive me back to Manhattan, but reluctantly agreed that we could go via the Bronx – as long as I did not try to get out of the car and would keep the door and window on my side locked. She pulled into a lay-by; the view was frightening: like illustrations for Dante's *Inferno* or newsreels from contemporary Aleppo. But it was not film or art work I was looking at; surrounded by ashy rubble which overlay and blotted out the street-plan were uninhabitable blackened apartment buildings with dazed people moving unbelievingly between them. The Grand Concourse had disappeared into the general ruination.

Tightrope Walkers

I do not blame my parents – both, I am sure, numbed by their own experience of the general indifference towards children when they were young. Certainly there were no reminiscences from either about their early days, no anecdotes of uncles, aunts or cousins, no proud recounting of adventures and triumphs: nothing at all. Their childhood images remain two small, pale, wary faces in old photographs.

My mother left her Austro-Hungarian village in the Kingdom of Galicia, aged about six, in the first years of the twentieth century: a time of political and social unrest and much anti-semitism, and with her family travelled across Europe from the eastern borders of the Hapsburg lands to their port of embarkation: Hamburg? Trieste? – sailing steerage class, I am fairly sure; to be confronted by a new country, a new language and all the shocks of the immigrant. But not a word was ever said to her children about what she had thought or felt. Not even a factual account of their route: what had happened on the way and how long the journey took, nor who had greeted them after their release from Ellis Island: she, her mother and her elder sister. Had the men of the family, the father and two much older brothers, also travelled with them or were they already in America? Or did they follow? (The sisters were under eight, the brothers over twenty years old.) It was impossible to get hard facts from my mother. I never knew her real age. She claimed either that the documents had been lost, or that such information had never been recorded. I knew that the bureaucracy of the Austro-Hungarian empire was excellent – but I never went to the trouble of trying to find her records, assuming they still existed. Perhaps the destruction of the wars that passed over her birthplace had belatedly made her story true. And it was only when it was too late to ask that I wanted to know more: everyone who could answer my questions was already dead.

Three of my four grandparents had died before I was born, and my father's father, who remarried twice after the death of his first wife, my father's mother, always lived in England, and in another town. I remember only a few of his visits; though retain a strong memory of how mercilessly he put me in my place as a female, and his expression of malicious pleasure at my fury as he recited (as he invariably did), 'Be good, sweet maid, and let who will be clever...' From the first moment, I was quite sure that clever was exactly what I wanted to be.

Until I was five years old we lived in New York City, but my father's family were all in London. It was two generations since his great-grandparents had left Cracow in the mid-nineteenth century, another time of revolutionary disturbance in Europe and much movement of people, and that was long ago enough for them to have lost all the characteristics of immigrants – in fact, to me they seemed to out-English the English. Trying now to interpret our first meeting, I have an uneasy memory of some difficulty related to my mother. Did her defensive immigrant nature make easy relationship impossible? But the matter was never discussed, even when I was an adult. And growing up in that family, I had never asked.

Of course I do not blame them. But I am suddenly conscious of being an instance of the impoverishment of family and memory that can result from such uprootings: left rigid with fear half-way across the tightrope of the present moment. No stories, no legends, nothing unique or special about us, about me, as protection against the pressure of the entire outside world, nothing except what I could create by the power of my own imagination.

Marranos

My aunt Ann had to wait until both her parents were dead before she could marry Roscoe. It would have been too much of a shock for them to know that their daughter was marrying a non-Jew. Not that my aunt was in any way observant: during the years of World War Two when we lived in her house, none of the High Holy Days was celebrated or even acknowledged. But in spite of her older sister's disapproval, my mother's determination to ensure that my brother and I did not forget that we were Jewish made her contact the local rabbi and arrange for us to attend the weekly *cheder* (which is what we called the Jewish Sunday school). I have no recollection of those classes, but somewhere there still might exist the certificate I gained for passing the first-year Hebrew test – although I quickly wiped what I had learned from my brain, because for as long as I remember I have not been able to read or understand a word of the language. The rabbi was young, and every few weeks I would go to his small modern apartment to babysit his two children (and examine the many interesting books on the bookshelves), while he and his pretty wife went out for the evening.

'The Jewish question' loomed large in our household. My aunt had stopped identifying herself as a Jew as soon as she and Roscoe left New York. It was not long before she succeeded in becoming a member of the local Ladies' Club, which was so important to her that, whenever our quarrels amplified into screaming matches, I would shout out the worst possible threat I could imagine: to reveal to everyone she knew that we were Jewish. Although the United States was part of the group of countries fighting the world's worst anti-Semite, in the state of Virginia in the 1940s, anti-Semitism – albeit a less murderous variety than in Europe – was rife.

It was in those years that I first learned about Queen Isabella and King Ferdinand of Spain, and the events of 1492: the triumph of Christianity and the expulsion of Moors and Jews from the Spanish peninsula, and Christopher Columbus's discovery of America funded by that same Spanish royal pair. I also learned about the Spanish Inquisition, and the horror of the torture and execution of those Jews and Muslims who chose to be burnt at the stake in the city's central square rather than renounce their religion and apostatise. Many Jews did convert to Christianity, but these 'conversos' or 'new Christians' or 'Marranos' were never really accepted. In my early twenties I lived for four years in Mallorca, and even then, centuries later, there was no problem in having Marrano families pointed out to me.

Learning about Marranos, while every day I could hear on the radio or read in my uncle's newspaper about the persecution of the Jews in Europe, and the fact that my aunt wanted to hide her Jewish identity, made it easy to imagine that now, centuries later, my mother and brother and I were in an almost comparable situation. It was frightening, and thrilling, because I knew that in fact I was quite safe, far from the war; that it was only my father who might be in danger.

My First Library

Aunt Ann, my mother's elder sister, was my mentor in everything to do with art, music, literature, and all things cultural. She arranged for me to go to Saturday morning art classes for schoolchildren at one of the city galleries, she introduced me to the opera broadcasts from the Metropolitan Opera House in New York which we listened to every Saturday afternoon when I got back home from the art class, and she took me to the local library to meet her friend the senior librarian, and thus opened the door to a treasure house: for although this was only a medium-sized suburban library, there seemed to be enough on its shelves to satisfy my curiosity about whatever in the world books promised to teach.

But the most important object my aunt gave me was the piece of furniture which represented the high altar of her religion of Culture: the deep-shelved, ornately carved, dark wood bookcase whose contents I began to investigate during those crucial few years when I was twelve and thirteen and fourteen years old and my mother and brother and I were living with Ann and her husband outside Washington D.C. during the Second World War. She told me proudly how she had saved up to buy it, after seeing it in an antique store near where she had worked in New York City as a young woman. The proprietor had agreed to keep it for her until she could pay its price. That bookcase is in my London sitting-room now and I have described it in a poem, 'Sugar-Paper Blue'.* I think the best way to give an idea of its significance to me is to quote the relevant lines:

> I was probably not more than twelve when,
> in my aunt's glass-fronted mahogany bookcase –
>> dusting its elaborate clawed feet,
>> the swagged garlands of leaves swathing
>> the hips of the female torsos that
>> surged from the columns each side
>> like naked caryatids, or
>> twin figureheads with the fixed eyes
>> and stern faces of implacable Fates
>> on the vessel of expectation
>> which that bookcase (the same piece now

in my London apartment; the one object
whose look and contents, I suspect,
formed my taste in everything) became –
I found what can only be called
'a slim volume', with limp covers,
in an unknown script and language.

What the soft-leather binding enclosed was a collection of poems
in Russian:

I don't remember Aunt Ann translating
one line from its pages, nor ever
explaining how she came to own it.
But she told me some facts about the woman
who wrote it – the first time I heard
those words: Anna Akhmatova –

I had been writing or composing poems in my head for a few years
already, but somehow, the existence of this mysterious volume, and
the fact that my aunt told me it was written by a woman, became
the confirmation of my identity as a poet: a fact I associate with
my aunt and have always been grateful for.

Every one of my aunt's tastes and range of interests was influential.
I remember reading, or attempting to read – obviously most of
these authors demanded a far greater knowledge of people, history,
and language than a girl of my age possessed: Boccaccio, Hemingway,
Thomas Mann (I don't know whether to laugh or cry when I
remember myself struggling through the first fifty or sixty pages
of *The Magic Mountain*; I did not return to it until I was in my
twenties); Chekhov and Maupassant: I loved their stories then and
still do; biographies of composers, painters, and heroic figures such
as T.E. Lawrence, Madame Curie and Dr. Schweitzer – and who
knows what else was on those shelves to feed my imagination?

The deep bottom shelf was filled with sheet music: my aunt's
girlhood ambition was to become an opera singer, and she still
had a thrilling contralto voice which seemed surprisingly powerful
coming from the throat of such a small woman. (She was also an
excellent whistler, and could imitate the songs of many birds.) I
would look at the pictures decorating the front of the scores of
popular songs and arias, read their words and try to work out how

the tunes sounded from the black and white notes along the staves
– but the idea of learning to play an instrument never came into
my thoughts nor was suggested by any adult. Now I think this
absence of expectation was evidence of the poverty of my aunt
and mother's childhood. Ann was extremely musical, and singing
was the only possible way she could express it. No expenditure
was required: the instrument was her own body.

The books I brought home from the public library – most of
them recommendations by the librarian, who introduced me to
standard English classics not part of my aunt's collection – were
further mental nourishment. How fortunate I was to have two
such cultivated women as mentors, and to have free access to the
fascinating and eclectic books that filled my aunt Ann's bookcase.

* 'Sugar-Paper Blue', *New & Collected Poems* (2010), p.414.

The Scratch

In winter there was a carpet on the floor, but at the start of summer, Uncle Roscoe would roll it back and heave it onto his shoulder, ends slowly sinking behind and before, and grinning like a Lascar stevedore, carry it to the cellar. The linoleum underneath had a wide border and tightly flowered centre printed in an old-fashioned formal design: Brussels carpet I think they called it, in a range of shades from cream through beige and brick and tan to darkest brown. I knew every flourish, repeat, and irregularity because once a week my task was to get down on my knees and wash the kitchen and also, in summer, the living-room floor. That was how I found it, a gouged-out crooked crescent inches long. The bearer of evil tidings, I might as well have been the guilty party. My house-proud aunt's distress was unnerving. To soothe her, and prove my innocence as well as my skill, I promised miracles.

Uncle Roscoe went down to his basement workbench to mix glue and putty, then tamped the ugly rip until it rose smooth and level. A box of oil paints had been my chosen birthday present. I squeezed dabs of umber and sienna, zinc white and cadmium yellow, from the smooth metal tubes onto the red-stained wooden palette and tentatively dragged streaks of pigment toward each other with a stiff new brush. I crouched, then knelt, then spread-eagled flat, licking sweat off my upper lip and wrinkling my nose to stop my glasses sliding. It took hours to match the colours and keep the paint within the limits of my uncle's repair, but I was pleased with what I had done.

All that August, during the hottest hours of afternoon, sunlight sifted through the screens like little heaps of still-warm white ash from last year's summer-camp fires. My brother and I would pull the curtains across every window in the living room to keep out the sun and sit cross-legged and barefoot on the cool linoleum, playing gin rummy. If you looked hard you could just see, like the stain left by a dropped twig or the shadow of a scar, the dull mark of the mended scratch on its patterned surface.

Goldenrod

In the empty lot opposite, the goldenrod. I walked down the porch steps and crossed the narrow road. Blossoming spikes reached as high as my shoulders, and as I pushed through them the loosened pollen made me sneeze.

Blue sky and gold flowers and pale dusty earth. Green leaves beginning to dry at the edges and curl inwards, rust-blotched by the close of summer. A space that seemed vast enough to hide from everything, among the densest clumps of bushes at the centre, to read and dream or watch how ants veered around the shiny pebbles, how beetles crawled up jointed grass stems and the mantis moved its legs. I had learned not to go barefoot because of the red chiggers that burrowed under the skin between your toes and had to be dug out. When I took my sandals off at night, the top of each foot was stained by the sun into an elaborate pattern of white and brown.

Now it was September, and I watched the goldenrod harden and darken. School had started a week ago and I was still in love with the same arrogant, bespectacled boy I had not seen since June. After class, we took up all our old arguments about God, Marx, and the meaning of life, just where we had left them, as if there had been no break. I had arrived home that afternoon so charged with refutations and unpresented evidence that I immediately sat down to write him a letter. I sealed the envelope and cut across the lot to the next street and the nearest mailbox. As soon as it had fallen through the slot I knew I had made a fool of myself.

The afternoon seemed even hotter than August, but maybe that was because I was wearing my new sloppy-joe sweater and pleated skirt instead of tee-shirt and shorts. There must be some way to get the letter back. If any neighbours passed they would be sure to ask why I was standing there. I retreated into the vegetation, keeping the box in my line of sight. The mailman was due about now. As I moved restlessly through them, drifts of disturbed pollen rose from the tall plants. But even after I explained why it was so important, he refused to let me search for my letter among the others. Nothing I said would sway him. He grinned and walked away muttering, 'Crazy kid!'

The dull yellow expanse of the field hummed and vibrated. In spite of the new school clothes I threw myself down on the hot ground between the bushes and later, blamed my swollen eyes and tear-streaked face on the powdery torment of the goldenrod.

The Dove Dress

Looking down at the printed pattern on the dull mauve fabric stretched across my knees, how much this dress reminds me of one I wore when twelve or thirteen years old. That also had an anachronistic style which made me feel in disguise: a dove-coloured nun rather than the adventurer I believed was my true nature, as if already, with my eighteenth-century imagination, I sensed an affinity between the two roles.

I bought this dress at a fashionable shop. The other had been a dress of my aunt's. By the time I claimed it, it might well have been twenty years old. The loose cotton, soft from being washed so often, was gathered into a deep yoke and the cuffs of wide puffed sleeves. Like this cloth, it was printed with small white blossoms. But there were touches of other colours, particularly the golden-apricot stroke along a petal of each flower, which I especially liked.

As a schoolgirl, on weekdays I dressed like everyone else: pleated woollen skirt, sloppy-joe sweater, sometimes buttoned down the back, with matching knee-high socks, and saddle-shoes (because, according to my aunt, moccasins didn't give enough support). But Saturday morning, and depending on the season wearing that dress more often than not, I took the bus from the corner of our street to a class for schoolchildren at the Corcoran Art Gallery in the city.

Those hours in the studio with its high skylight, the air dusty with charcoal and pastel, scented by fixative, thick with the silence of concentration, were one of the best times of the week. Afterwards, if there wasn't a broadcast from the Metropolitan Opera that Saturday, I went downstairs to the main galleries. When the shadowy room of plaster casts of famous statues was empty, I would sit down and try to draw one of them. That day I had positioned myself against the plinth of a conveniently placed gladiator and started to rough-in the forms of Rodin's *The Kiss* on a clean leaf of my sketch pad.

'That's pretty good.' I heard a soft Southern murmur over my shoulder, and turned to meet the gaze of a slight youth in military uniform, whose velvety stubble of dark hair made me feel a disturbing combination of repulsion and the desire to rub the palm of my hand across it.

My friends could read the signs that indicated rank, but I had never managed to absorb the information. Neither was I good at judging age, though he did not seem much older than the senior boys at school. Flattered by his comment, I was troubled by the problem of how to reply. As often before (and since), I thought how much more satisfactory it is to imagine something happening than to be presented with the actuality. 'You really can draw,' he continued. 'I wish I could draw like that. Does it come naturally, or do you have lessons?'

Now he had asked a question I could tell him about the classes. Talking made me feel less awkward. 'Are you interested in art?' Of course he had come to the gallery, but I did not have high expectations of soldiers. They were necessary to fight wars, I knew well enough – otherwise I equated them with the sort of young men who got drunk and whistled at girls, made jokes about niggers and Yids, and guffawed when the word 'art' was mentioned.

'I guess I am interested,' he admitted. His uncertainty increased my confidence. I twirled a lock of hair forward and pushed my glasses up my nose. 'I'm going to be an artist. I'll probably go to Paris to study, after the war.'

'You're really cute, you know that?' I saw no connection between being cute and being an artist, and the flush that mounted my face confused and angered me. 'This is a famous statue,' I stated decisively. The yearning figures glowed whitely. He looked down at my drawing. 'Would you let your boyfriend kiss you like that?'

It was easy to avoid the trap he was setting. 'Oh, I just started to draw this one because our teacher was talking about it today.'

He changed the subject. 'You look like a real artist. That's the sort of dress I always imagined an artist would wear.'

'I'll have to go now. My aunt is waiting for me.'

'I was going to invite you for an ice-cream soda.' He sounded disappointed. I remember thinking how jealous my friends would be when I told them.

The dark and silent gallery with its varnished panelling, the pale greasy gleam of plaster like dough gone hard, and two young people seen small and distant: he with his short cap of furry hair and olive drab uniform and she in the dove-coloured dress which she stripped off and threw into the back of the closet as soon as she got home – is what this new dress evokes.

Rover

The two houses stood stranded between the last street where whites lived and the beginning of the black district: a no-man's zone of empty lots and decrepit farmsteads whose fields had been sold off decades before. The town was already jammed with army people and war-workers when my uncle was sent there to supervise a new factory. Suddenly, for the duration of the war, he had become head of a family consisting not only of himself and his wife but also his wife's sister and her two children. Finding anywhere at all to live was a stroke of luck, so he had bought one of the badly-built pair. The other was occupied by Walter and Dolly, their baby boy, daughter Diana, and Rover, the red setter dog. Not yet thirty years old, the couple already looked slack and middle-aged.

My aunt soon developed a maternal attitude to the younger woman. 'She doesn't know how to look after a family, poor girl. I guess her mother never taught her.' Wearing the starched house-dress of flowered cotton, sleeves and neck modestly decorated with coloured rickrack, which she changed into after coming home from the office, my aunt was the picture of domestic efficiency. She would praise Diana until I burned with jealousy. 'A little angel. To think she's cursed with a father like that.' Walter was a policeman. He kept guns in the house and did target practice in the basement, bet on horses, and spent the weekend drinking beer and shouting, first effusively and then more and more irritably, at wife, children, and dog. As the Saturday evening sky darkened, Dolly's expression became nervous and placatory. She would pull the children towards her, then hurry them to bed out of Walter's way.

Though two years younger than my brother, and half my age, Diana pleaded to join in everything we did. There was no one else for her to play with. When her father was home, she came to us to avoid him. I knew it hurt her even more than Dolly must have been hurt, when Walter shouted and slapped her mother's face. Silently, Dolly would lift a hand to the livid mark down one cheek as if to soothe and hide it, and stare with wide eyes at her balding, tense-featured husband. 'Why don't you say something, you stupid fat cow?' I heard him scream one Saturday afternoon.

It was a particularly hot summer, and the coolest place to be was the cellar. Dirty and barefoot, wearing the minimum allowed, the three of us sat on the wooden steps leading down from the kitchen, or on the half-broken wicker chairs near the galvanised iron wash-tubs, planning the rules of our secret club and the fearsome initiation rites Diana must undergo if she wanted to become a member. Her dark blonde hair curled damply around her worried, excited little face as she listened. We were too timid, or perhaps too soft-hearted, to subject her to those comic-book inspired ordeals, but enjoyed tormenting her with vivid descriptions of what lay in store.

There was an epidemic of rabies in town, and one oppressive morning, Rover began to run in circles around the back yard making strange laboured sounds rather than barking, as white foam fell in large flakes from open jaws onto the burnt, straw-pale grass and the sweat-darkened red of his coat. Dolly called us into the house and latched the screen door shut. My brother knelt on a chair so that he could look over the window sill, then turned to me, eyes piteous, a greyish pattern of mesh on his nose and forehead where they had pressed against the screen, and asked, 'They won't kill him, will they?'

It was not long before a patrol car arrived and Walter and a colleague, bizarre paunchy figures in their sombre uniforms, emerged and walked carefully across the yard through the shimmering midday heat. The moment they came into the house, the baby began to cry, and my brother tugged at Walter's arm, demanding, 'What are you going to do to Rover?' Walter looked hot and uneasy and about to lose his temper. 'That dog is sick, understand? He's a very dangerous animal. If he bit any of you kids you'd die. It would take a long time and it would hurt a lot.'

'Can't you make him better?' my brother insisted. 'I'll look after him. I'll feed him every day and give him water. I won't forget, you won't have to keep after me.' 'Leave me alone.' Walter shrugged his arm away and went into the bedroom. A few moments later he re-appeared, breaking and loading a rifle. In spite of Dolly's efforts, the baby was still screaming. Diana and my brother moved closer together, and closer to Dolly. 'Now stop it, all of you,' Walter commanded. 'That dog has got to be killed. It's a danger to everyone, and only a sissy would make a fuss.'

The screen door slammed behind him. No one moved until we

heard the first shot, and then another immediately after. Rover had not made a sound. The baby fell silent as Diana and my brother began to cry, and her sobs and his muffled choking almost obscured the sound of the police car driving away.

The Graduation Dress

Two Box-Brownie snapshots, deckle-edged, over-exposed or faded to greyish sepia, family-album sized: copies, I'm sure, of prints mailed to my father, during the war.

That damned war, which my mother insisted had destroyed our family.

One of the photos is of my brother and me, the other of the three of us. We are standing on a wide stretch of lawn at the front of the school building, and it was probably taken by the helpful parent of a class-mate, to commemorate my graduation from Thomas Jefferson Junior High School in early June 1944.

The collar of Harry's short-sleeved shirt is buttoned and his hands are clasped behind his back. He wears long trousers for the occasion, and his expression is serious and proud. He wants his father to see what a big boy he is for a nine-year old. My mother's head tilts to one side at its characteristic wistful angle, haloed by the brim of a straw hat. The soft frills at the neckline of her printed dress continue to the waist, and her hands are encased in pale net gloves. She is gazing intently out of the picture, as though determined to meet and hold the eyes of her husband across the thousands of miles which separated them.

I had realised by then that I was no longer a child, but am surprised by how mature I appear: taller than my mother – already full height at the age of thirteen – an attractive girl with curly shoulder-length dark hair drawn back from a high forehead, holding a rolled diploma in my left hand, a corsage of flowers (which my aunt had bought for me) pinned at the same shoulder. I must have just taken off my glasses so as not to be photographed wearing them: the explanation for my sultry, unfocussed myopic gaze.

I can recall every detail of my special costume for the graduation ceremony, from the unaccustomed thick feel and rustling sound of nylon stockings rubbing against each other as I moved, to the traditional white dress, which I had made myself. As usual, nothing available from the local stores conformed to the clear image in my mind of how I wanted to look: which was why I made most of what I wore at that time. I admired the elaborate iron latticework of my aunt's old treadle sewing machine, and enjoyed sitting there, pumping my legs up and down, watching the seamed cloth flow away from under the forked foot and flashing, stabbing needle.

The fabric I chose, a slithery rayon, was quite unsuitable for the style of dress, which had a panelled princess cut, square neck and short sleeves. Equally inappropriate was the thin black velvet ribbon trimming. It was a difficult and unsatisfying piece of dressmaking and, as if under a magnifying glass, I can still see the marks left in the cloth by pins and unpicked stitching, the grubby, too-often handled binding of the neck and sleeves and the tangled threads inside where seams had already begun to fray.

It is easy to remember those hopeless moments when everything seemed to go wrong; yet studying the photograph now, the dress looks perfectly acceptable, and the smooth young face of the girl who wears it is as closed and mysterious as a stranger's.

Malted Milk

The thick sweetness of malted milk was the flavour of those mornings when I would sit with my current best friend at the soda-fountain in the corner drugstore and share a milkshake before another day at T.J. Junior High. I remember her sallow serious face with the cowed expression of a daughter of Jehovah's Witnesses, and going with her family once to the wooden chapel where their congregation worshipped – although I have entirely forgotten her name.

Almost forty years later I was trying to find that drugstore, that school, the vacant lot we cut across on our way home every afternoon, and the house or even just the street where my mother, brother and I had lived with Aunt Ann and Uncle Roscoe.

The row of modest houses we had moved to after being Dolly and Walter's neighbours, jerry-built for an influx of war workers, which ours began or ended (depending where you started), the derelict farmhouse nearby with its yard full of broken machinery, the scrubby tract of ground behind half-dead trees where my friends and I imagined rapists lurked, and the unexplored region beyond: all return in meticulous detail. But the name of the street and the number of the house escaped me, and studying the local map was little help. I recognised the main thoroughfares: Glebe Road, Columbia Pike, Wilson Boulevard – but none of the intersecting gridwork between struck more or less familiar. The schools we went to during the war (I mean the Second World War, not those other wars their names evoke: Thomas Jefferson Junior High, Patrick Henry Elementary, Washington-Lee High) were still marked, and I thought they might be a start.

Outside the Metro station, nothing gave a clue about which direction to take. It was a cold bright morning. I craved the comfort of sugar, the support of malted milk, but could not see a cafe or drugstore, only a row of telephone booths near a DIY warehouse. The best idea seemed to call for a taxi. Ten minutes later a low caramel-coloured car pulled up. The driver had the broken-veined complexion and wistful expression of a drinker. Neither he nor his car were in their prime.

I knew it would be hard to explain what I wanted, but hadn't expected him to state with such assurance that T.J. wasn't there any more, nor the High School either. 'I used to go to those schools,' I protested, adding, 'I haven't been back since then,' as though if I could gain his interest and sympathy he might conjure them back into existence.

'You went to Washington-Lee?' He turned to get a better look at me. 'The old building was beat up by the time I got there. Wore out by kids. That must have been – when was it? – about '53.' I realised that his eyes were a beautiful blue, and that he was the younger. 'Just before I went into the Marines.' 'And I've been away for years.' How lucky that he had come in answer to my call, rather than another driver. 'I think T.J.'s a sort of community center now.' We cruised past a row of stores that must have been there then. A shabby movie house looked familiar, and the drug-store on the corner we were turning. 'I think I recognise that.' I felt ridiculously excited. 'Sure, we all hung out round there, but they took away the soda fountain years ago.'

'Do you remember Smoky Hollow?' I wondered if it was a good idea to ask. The ones my aunt wanted me to be friends with avoided the place, but I was sure he had known it well: a sandy depression in a weed-grown field behind the playground where certain people would go when they cut class to drink from hip-flasks, smoke pot, and make and change relationships of love and power. The driver nodded. Through the rear mirror I saw the corner of his mouth curve, as though he didn't smile often. 'It's just a truck-park now. Nothing left of Smoky Hollow.'

A half-constructed underpass blocked the direct route. Not much of the old High School had survived extension and alteration. He walked around the site with me, then shook his head disbelievingly. 'I live in this town, but I just hadn't realised.'

We circled and quartered the area. Only a few houses of the appropriate age and style still stood. Most of the buildings were new red-brick low-income apartment blocks. Even the street plan had altered from what the driver remembered. I chose a house almost at random.

There was no problem in placing my aunt's pots of blackish-purple and pale yellow pansies along each side of the paved path or up the concrete steps to the front door, and the little porch at the back, with the garbage cans underneath, could easily have been

101

the eyrie where I'd brooded about my future. On the other side of that white-painted dormer window might be the same room Mother and I had shared. But looking at the photographs I took then, I am not convinced. It is more disconcerting to think I passed the house and did not recognise it than to accept that it had been demolished.

The driver hunched in his seat smoking while I prowled with my camera. 'Where to?' he asked as I got back into the car. I felt jaded and irritable. 'I'd like a malted milk. Will you have one with me?'

'Sorry, lady. I've got another job waiting. But I'm obligated to you. Otherwise I probably wouldn't ever know that it isn't like it was.'